Where the Wild Horses Roam

DOROTHY HINSHAW PATENT

Where the Wild Horses Roam

PHOTOGRAPHS BY

WILLIAM MUÑOZ

CLARION BOOKS

NEW YORK

ACKNOWLEDGMENTS: The author and photographer wish to thank Jerry Jack, Phyllis Falconer, Fred Wyatt, Carol Brauner, and Joey Deeg for their help with this book. Special thanks go to Lynn Taylor, for all the time he gave us, and for reading and commenting on the manuscript.

All photographs in this book are by William Muñoz except the following by Dorothy Hinshaw Patent, pages 26 (bottom); 28; 48.

Clarion Books
a Houghton Mifflin Company imprint
52 Vanderbilt Avenue, New York, NY 10017
Text copyright © 1989 by Dorothy Hinshaw Patent
Photographs copyright © 1989 by William Muñoz

For information about permission to reproduce selections from this book, write to Permissions, Houghton Mifflin Company, 2 Park Street, Boston, MA 02108

Book Design by Sylvia Frezzolini
Printed in the U.S.A.
Library of Congress Cataloging-in-Publication Data
Patent, Dorothy Hinshaw.   Where the wild horses roam
by Dorothy Hinshaw Patent; photographs by William Muñoz.
p. cm. Includes index.
Summary: Text and photographs present a history of wild horses in this country, the mistreatment they have suffered, and the efforts that have been made to protect them by law.
ISBN 0-89919-507-5 : $15.95
1. Wild horses—United States—Juvenile literature. [1. Wild horses. 2. Horses. 3. Wildlife management.] I. Muñoz, William, ill. II. Title
SF360.3.U6P38 1989   88-20360
639.9′79725—dc19   CIP
                                                              AC

Y   10 9 8 7 6 5 4 3 2 1

For all those who truly love horses
and work for their welfare
and humane treatment.

Contents

Chapter One

WILD AND FREE

Sniffing the breeze, the wild stallion held his head high as he trotted over the soft grass. His nose told him there were mares at the spring below, and the urge to join them was strong. He had almost reached the other horses when he stopped in his tracks — a sturdy, high fence blocked his path. He trotted along it, and looked for a way to get to the mares, but the fence surrounded them. He was free, but they were captives. Then he caught another scent and snorted in alarm. Two humans, unaware of his presence, were walking his way. Just as the people spotted the stallion, he tossed his wild, tangled mane, wheeled around, and galloped quickly away from the pens of captured wild mares.

Today, roundups across the West bring more and more wild horses into captivity. Some people fear that this symbol of freedom will disappear from the land. But others are glad to know that there are fewer wild ones drinking scarce water and eating what little food is available for cattle and wildlife.

HORSES RETURN TO AMERICA

Wild horses and Indian ponies are such a part of American western history that it is hard to believe they didn't always roam the West. The early evolution of the horse took place in America. But over eight thousand years ago, after spreading across the Bering Strait land bridge in the Far North to Asia and Europe, horses died out on the American continent. When the Spanish explorers came to Mexico in the fifteenth century, they brought horses with them. As the Spanish moved northward into the American West, their hardy horses made conquest and settlement possible. The native Indians had no horses as galloping mounts from which to battle the Spaniards and quickly lost out to them in war.

The Spanish settlers enslaved the Indians in the Southwest, forcing them to farm for them and to be servants. Although the slaves helped care for the horses and other livestock, they were not allowed to learn to ride horses. But the Indians could see how useful horses were. They watched carefully and soon mastered the art of riding.

Once the Indians knew how to use them, horses spread northward among the tribes by theft, trading, and the capture of escaped horses gone wild.

Thus, the first American wild horses of modern times were Spanish horses that got loose. The horses survived well on their own and multiplied rapidly. More escaped from the Indian tribes that had acquired them from the settlers. These early Spanish horses are often referred to

Wild horses.

as *mustangs*. They were small, tough horses, surefooted and good at working with cattle. Their backs were shorter than those of most horses, with one less bone, or vertebra, in the backbone.

As settlers from the eastern United States moved across the western prairies during the 1800s, they also took horses with them. But their horses, which had been brought to America by immigrants from northern Europe, were different. They had riding horses that were generally taller than the mustangs and work horses that were heavier. Some of these animals, too, went wild when their owners gave up the hardships of farming and returned east or when pioneers died of famine or

disease. These animals bred with the mustangs, changing the nature of the American wild horse.

Today some people use the term *mustang* interchangeably with *wild horse*. But others object, saying that only those horses with the physical characteristics of the original Spanish horses should be called mustangs.

WILD WEST DAYS

About two million wild horses roamed across the western deserts in the early nineteenth century. Herds of thousands grazed peacefully, disturbed only by wolves and by the occasional raids of Indians or settlers looking

Once thousands of wild horses like these roamed the West.

for hardy mounts. But as pioneers settled the West, the wide open spaces began to disappear. Fences enclosed private property, and towns dotted the landscape. Farmers cultivated land for crops. Ranchers let their cattle range over government lands. There was less and less room for wanderers like the Indians, bison, and wild horses.

The majority of Indians today live on reservations. Most of their lands have been taken over, and many tribes were forced to move into unfamiliar territory as white settlement progressed. The enormous herds of wandering bison are gone. Bison now are restricted to limited parks and preserves where they are carefully

Wild horses run free in open spaces.

managed. All that is left of the "Wild" West are the wild horses that know no property lines, no boundaries. These hardy creatures have become a symbol of the pioneer days of our country. Just knowing that they still run free lifts the spirits of city dwellers who may never see the grandeur of western mountains and deserts.

Despite the romantic appeal of wild horses, the general public was unconcerned about them until quite recently. Before 1971, the fate of the wild horses depended completely on the attitudes of the people who lived around them. Ranchers used them as a handy resource, taking young horses to be tamed as riding animals. Often the ranchers would free large stallions

among the wild bands to increase the size of the new foals so they would be strong enough to work with cattle.

In such areas, the ranchers and the wild horses shared the land in relative harmony. But in some other regions, people lacked respect for the wild animals. They saw them as a source of ready cash and rounded them up in large numbers to be sent to pet-food factories.

WILD HORSE ANNIE

The wild horse preservation movement began with a tough and determined woman named Velma Johnston. Mrs. Johnston lived on a ranch twenty-six miles from Reno, Nevada, during the 1940s. At that time, the United States had no laws to protect wild horses. Pilots in low-flying, small airplanes buzzed the horses and frightened them into running toward waiting captors. The horses were run to exhaustion, making them too worn out to resist being loaded into trucks that would take them to slaughter. The trips were long, and the horses often were not fed or watered along the way. They were thought of as money on the hoof, not as living creatures that could feel pain.

One day in 1950, while driving to work in Reno, Mrs. Johnston found herself behind a truck full of bleeding, injured wild horses. The sight disturbed her so much that she followed the truck instead of going to her job. As the suffering animals were unloaded to be slaughtered, she took pictures of them. That was the beginning of her crusade for the humane treatment of wild horses.

From then until her death in 1977, Mrs. Johnston worked for wild horses. She founded two organizations devoted to preserving them and helped bring about the federal laws that now govern their treatment and management. During her campaign, she took on the nickname "Wild Horse Annie," originally coined as a joke by a government official who didn't take her seriously. The first law that resulted from Mrs. Johnston's efforts was dubbed the "Wild Horse Annie law." Passed in 1959 by Congress, it forbade the use of airplanes and motorized vehicles like cars and trucks to round up wild horses. It also made the poisoning of water holes to capture the animals illegal.

Unfortunately, the Wild Horse Annie law was difficult to enforce. Few people lived on the vast western deserts, and it was easy for lawbreakers to round up the horses unnoticed. Often, officials paid little attention to what was going on. But by the 1960s, thousands of Americans had become concerned with the plight of the wild horses. The government was forced to respond to this strong public sentiment.

*Much of the land where wild horses live is desert,
like this area of Wyoming.*

In 1971, the Wild Horse and Burro Act was passed by Congress. This law completely changed the status of wild horses and burros (also called donkeys). Like horses, donkeys had escaped from captivity and lived successfully in the wild. Managing these creatures on most federal lands became the job of the government. No longer could private citizens enter these areas and remove wild horses or burros. The animals were protected by law.

A wild stallion with his band.

Chapter Two

LIVING WILD

Even though they have different ancestries and live in many places, wild horses everywhere behave in very similar ways. When water is scarce or when the horses are crowded, they may become more aggressive than normal. And in areas where they are used to humans, they may be less "wild" than in regions where people are scarce. But, generally, wild horse behavior in Nevada, Montana, Oregon, or wherever the horses may roam is very much alike.

FAMILY LIFE

Horses are social creatures. Like humans, they seek the company of their own kind. A wild horse "family," called a *band* or *harem,* is made up of one stallion and at least one mare. Some stallions command harems with six or more mares, and a few bands have more than one stallion. In the spring, the foals are born, usually during the night or at dawn. Foals can stand up and walk soon after being born. Before long, they are running with the rest of the family. The young horses remain with the band until they are two or three years old.

Mares born into the band leave when they are old enough to breed. Stallions that are ready to start their own harems are attracted to the young mares. A young stallion may try to "steal" a mare away from her family. This is one way he can start his own band. Sometimes, mares wander away from their bands. Then a stallion may find her, starting his harem that way.

The stallions are always alert to the presence of one another since stallions are ever ready to add mares to their harems. Whenever a stallion comes across a pile of manure, he sniffs at it carefully. If the manure is from another stallion, he may add his own deposit to the pile, showing that he was there, too. Such "stallion piles" can become large and obvious, especially at important places such as near a water hole or along well-used trails.

A foal nurses.

Top: *The stallions are usually gentle with the foals.*
Bottom: *A stallion sniffs a manure pile.*

THE CHALLENGE OF THE STALLIONS

In the springtime, after the foals conceived the year before are born, the mares are ready to mate again. This is the time stallions are most likely to fight over mares. A young bachelor may challenge an older harem stallion. The two animals sniff at each other and let out loud, short whinnies. They arch their necks and prance back and forth, lifting their legs gracefully. They stamp the ground, pawing at the earth with their hooves.

Chances are the two horses already know one another. They have met and perhaps fought before, so each knows the other's strength. Usually, the challenge ends with the younger horse turning away. But if he has become stronger during the past year or if he senses that the older stallion is weaker than before, he may refuse to leave. Then a real fight may take place.

The two horses rear up on their hind legs and kick out with their front legs. If this gesture does not settle the fight, the horses bite each other. The stallions drop to their knees to avoid potentially crippling leg bites. The fight continues, with biting, kicking, and whinnying, until one horse has had enough and runs away. The other stallion chases after him, bumping against his body and kicking at him with his hind legs.

While a battle between two wild stallions may look

Above: *One stallion challenges another.*

Left: *The two animals rear up.*

Above: *Stallions often kick during fights.*
Below: *A winner chases away a loser.*

quite fierce, it usually ends with injuries from bites and kicks that will heal over time. The bodies of wild stallions are marked by the scars of many battle wounds. Sometimes, however, a wound can become infected. A horse with an infected leg wound or broken teeth may die because it cannot easily get enough food.

Since they need a lot of strength and experience to acquire mares, stallions usually do not succeed in starting a harem until they are five or six years old. Younger stallions join together in their own all-male bands. One becomes the leader of the other stallions, much as he later will manage his family of mares and foals. Older stallions that have lost out to strong, young ones may become loners. They often challenge other stallions over mares, even though they rarely win. From the time he becomes an adult until he dies, a stallion's life revolves around the possession of mares.

STAYING WELL FED

Like other wild animals, the horses must devote most of their time to getting enough food and water. A horse needs to consume about twenty-five pounds of grass each day to stay healthy. In order to take in that much food, wild horses spend half of their time grazing, heads down to the ground, nipping off mouthfuls of grass. The

Above: *A bachelor band.*

Right: *Wild horses spend many hours grazing each day.*

stallion usually grazes a little apart from his mares, putting himself between them and possible danger or other stallions. For example, if the band is grazing near the top of a hill, the stallion may graze closest to the top. The horses can see the lower slopes well, but could be surprised by animals coming over the hill.

Horses usually drink once or twice a day, depending on how hot the weather is. But where water is scarce and distant from pastures, the horses may only drink every other day. When thirsty, the band quits grazing

At the water hole.

and heads toward the well-worn paths that lead to water. Often the mares and foals drink first while the stallion, head up and alert for danger, stands guard. After the rest of the band has drunk its fill, the stallion takes his turn. Then the horses return to the pastures to graze. The bands in any one area take turns at the watering hole. A band with a more dominant stallion drinks first. In areas where water is scarce, a band with a weaker stallion may have a hard time getting enough to drink.

Young stallions taking a bath. Wild horses enjoy water baths and dust baths, which help control biting insects that bother them.

PROTECTING THEMSELVES

Wild horses have no natural enemies except for an occasional mountain lion. But the horses' instinct for preservation has remained intact through the generations, and the stallion always keeps an eye out for anything unusual. If a human appears on the horizon, he swings up his head, sniffs the air, and takes a few steps forward. He trots one way in front of the mares, turns, and trots back again. He gives a warning, taking in air quickly and letting it out with a loud snort. When the

mares hear that sound, they lift up their heads. They face the intruder and stare, ready to take flight in an instant. The stallion usually decides when to flee. He trots toward the mares, swinging his head low, and they run off, often led by an older, wise female. The stallion takes up the rear, ready to turn and face the danger if necessary.

Some stallions are more protective than others. While one may let people get close to his family without showing concern, another stampedes his mares at the sight of a distant human.

A stallion stands between his band and possible danger.

The band is alerted.

This stallion is urging his mares to move more quickly by lowering his head and holding his ears back.

ON THEIR OWN

Even though their ancestors were tended by humans for thousands of years, wild horses manage to take care of themselves very well. No one is there to bring them hay in the winter or to attend the births of their foals. Yet the horses not only survive in the wild, they thrive there. Wild horses in America have been multiplying rapidly since the Wild Horse and Burro Act was passed in 1971. Their very success has become a problem for them and for those responsible for their management.

Chapter Three

TOO MANY HORSES?

Horses roam free today in ten western states. More than half of the wild horses live in Nevada, where 86 percent of the land is publicly owned. Wyoming has the second largest population of wild horses, followed by Oregon, California, and Utah. Small numbers are found in Idaho, Colorado, Arizona, Montana, and New Mexico.

No one knows for sure how many wild horses roamed public lands in the West in 1971 when the Wild Horse and Burro Act was passed. The official estimate places the number at about seventeen thousand, but many knowledgeable people believe there were more. The number of horses had been kept down by people harvesting them for riding or for sale. But once they came under government protection, the wild horses were free to multiply. By 1980, the estimated wild horse population had grown to sixty-four thousand. Where horses, cattle, and wildlife shared the land, many people became concerned that overpopulation of grazing animals was damaging the feeding grounds.

THE WILD HORSE AS AN INVADER

The wild horse is actually misnamed. It isn't "wild" by the true definition of the word, something that has never been tamed. All the "wild" horses in America today are descended from tame animals that escaped or were set free. The correct technical term for such animals is *feral,* which means domesticated animals that have gone wild.

So, like the domesticated cow, which originated in Europe, the horse is not a natural part of the American environment. Natural communities of plants and animals have evolved together over the ages so that they remain in balance. The plant eaters do not consume all the plants, and the number of animals is regulated by the other animals that prey on them.

When humans interfere with nature, the natural balance can be upset. In America, humans have eliminated some important species. For example, wolves once preyed on plant eaters such as the moose, elk, deer, and antelope that live in thc West. But the wolves also attacked domesticated animals, so people killed off these predators. Without wolves, the wild animals wolves once hunted can become overpopulated. In most areas, hunters are allowed to harvest such species, so

they stay under control. But in parks such as Yellowstone, where hunting is not allowed, overpopulation of large plant eaters has become a problem because their major predator, the wolf, is gone.

When an outside species is introduced, it too can throw off the natural balance. Wild horses reproduce very quickly. In a good year, most foals survive and, by their second year, a few young female horses already bear foals of their own, although most don't bear young for at least another year. From the time she is five until seventeen years of age, a healthy mare will give birth almost every year. Since wild horses have virtually no natural enemies, only disease and starvation can keep their numbers down without human intervention. For these reasons, the population of wild horses doubles in four to seven years if it is left alone.

Because wild horses multiply so quickly and are not a natural part of the environment, managing them is very important. Too many horses means too many mouths to feed and too many hooves trampling tender, young grasses. In each area where they live, the number of horses must somehow be regulated. Otherwise the animals can cause real damage to the range.

In many areas where cattle and sheep, the other intruding species, are grazed, they are kept off the public lands during the winter and spring. They are only put

Both these foals are likely to survive to adulthood.

out to pasture after the grasses have grown strong and tall. But the wild horses stay all year-round. They are hungry in the springtime and eat the tender, young shoots of grass that first emerge from the cold soil. When there are too many horses, the grass is cut back by the horses' sharp teeth whenever it puts out new growth.

Grass is sparse in much of wild horse country.

Eventually, the plants die. When the grass dies, there isn't food later on in the year for the horses, cattle, elk, or bighorn sheep that depend on it. And without plant roots to hold it together, the soil can easily be washed or blown away. It takes only a few years to damage the land seriously through overgrazing. But it takes a very long time to rebuild it after the harm has been done.

When wild horses gallop across dry land, their hooves cut into the ground, raising clouds of dust.

MANAGING WILD HORSES

The public lands on which the federal government manages wild horses are under the control of the Bureau of Land Management, or BLM. Ranchers pay the BLM for "grazing rights," which allow them to graze a certain number of livestock on public lands. Much of that land is quite barren, and water is often scarce. As wild horse numbers increased, ranchers complained that the horses were eating too much grass and drinking too much water and were competing with their cattle. They said that the horses were even chasing cows away from water troughs in very dry areas.

It is hard to know just how much damage wild horses have been doing to public rangelands. On the average, wild horses consume less than 10 pecent of the available food, and wildlife eats only about 5 percent. That leaves 85 percent for livestock. Thus, on the whole, too many cattle rather than too many wild horses are probably responsible for overgrazing in many places. However, while most areas have many more cows than horses, others have more wild horses than cattle. For this reason, the horses may well be a problem in certain areas, especially in dry areas where plants grow slowly.

Because wild horses multiply so fast and because they can damage the range, the number of wild horses does

These cattle are being driven through a wild horse refuge and cannot stay. But in other areas, the wild horses must share the land with cattle.

need to be controlled. Besides, the law only allows wild horses in areas where they were living in 1971, when the Wild Horse and Burro Act was passed. Many people are working to find solutions to these population problems that will satisfy the majority of those concerned about wild horses.

The rugged beauty of the Pryor Mountain Wild Horse Range.

Chapter Four

A REFUGE FOR MUSTANGS

One solution to the wild horse population problem is to set aside refuges for the horses. On such refuges, the horses wouldn't have to compete with cattle for food. While native wildlife is always taken into consideration on public lands, any decisions about how many horses could roam on a refuge would be made with the welfare of the horses in mind.

Despite the concern about wild horses, only a small number live on land reserved for them. The first refuge for wild horses was set aside in Nevada in 1961. Its 395,000 acres are part of the Nellis Air Force Bombing Range. While today over a thousand wild horses roam the mountains and deserts of the refuge, people are not allowed in the area to see the horses because the air force still uses the region for military purposes. In western Colorado, about 28,000 acres were reserved in 1980 for wild horses that had roamed the area for generations. This refuge, called the Little Book Cliff Wild Horse Range, is home to 80 to 100 wild horses. The best-known wild horse refuge, however, is in Montana.

PROTECTED MUSTANGS

The rugged Pryor Mountain Wild Horse Range in southern Montana, set aside in 1968, is the home of about 120 wild horses. This 44,000-acre region of red desert, towering cliffs, and high mountain meadows is not much good for anything but hardy, surefooted animals. The brushy Dryhead area of the range receives only about five inches of rain each year. It harbors more bare soil than clumps of grass and can support only 31 horses. The steep, partially wooded slopes of Sykes ridge and Tillett ridge are home to about 45 horses each. Along the ridge tops, over a mile and a quarter above sea level, the upper meadows of the refuge catch the rain from passing clouds and provide summer pastures for many of the Tillett and Sykes ridge horses.

*A stallion in the
Dryhead area.*

*The grassy upper meadows
provide summer food for
many of the Pryor
Mountain horses.*

SPECIAL HORSES

The Pryor Mountain horses are a handsome bunch. Colors only rarely seen in domesticated horses are common in these bands, with many glossy blacks mingling with striking buckskins and unusual horses called *grullas*. Grullas are like buckskins in that their manes, tails, and lower legs are a darker shade than the rest of the body. But instead of being shaded in brown like buckskins, grullas are tones of blue-black. Many of the

This young grulla foal has zebra stripes on its legs and dark markings across its shoulders.

Pryor buckskins and grullas have striking zebra stripes along the backs of their legs. They usually sport a dark line extending down the back from the mane to the tail and often have dark markings across their shoulders.

The colors of these horses are characteristic of the early Spanish mustangs. Because of their special colors and their compact bodies, the Pryor Mountain horses are thought by some people to have descended largely from the original Spanish horses.

The stallion on the left is a buckskin; on the right is a dark grulla. The colors of both are typical of Pryor Mountain horses.

MANAGING THE HORSES

Because the land on the Pryor Mountain Wild Horse Range is so dry and unproductive, managing the horses to keep their numbers under control is very important. The population can increase quickly. After a hard winter, only seventy horses survived on the range in 1978. But by 1982, there were already 180 horses in the Pryors. In 1973, the Adopt-a-Horse program was started at the Pryor refuge. The horses that were removed from the range were made available to the public for adoption.

At first, roundups were held to remove horses when the population got too large — in 1973, 1975, 1977, and 1982. Now roundups are usually held every year to keep the number of horses as close to the ideal of 121 as possible. Since twenty to thirty foals are born each year, about that many horses must be removed during the roundup. Before the horses are gathered, the ones to be adopted are carefully selected. Mares and stallions of different ages and some foals are chosen. The best horses are left on the range so that the Pryor herd retains the most colorful horses with the straightest legs and best hooves. Sometimes a horse is moved from one area of the range to another if it has desirable traits needed there.

Some of the horses are rounded up by riders on

The cowboys head out to round up the horses.

horseback and roped. Others are captured at watering holes. The hole is surrounded by a fence with a gate that is left open most of the time. During the roundup, the gate is closed while the band is drinking. Then the horses that will be removed are taken to the roundup corrals at the end of a rope. A paved road runs through the Dryhead area, so horses rounded up there are loaded

At the end of the afternoon, a Pryor mustang is taken to the roundup pens at the end of a rope.

into a horse trailer and driven to the corrals at another part of the refuge, where they will be kept until they are adopted.

The horses taken from the Pryors find homes easily. Many people are happy to provide a home for a wild horse. This method of dealing with the excess animals worked so well at the Pryors that it has been used since 1976 in all areas where the BLM is removing horses from the wild.

Sometimes the horses are roped during the roundup.

Thousands of wild horses live in Nevada.

Chapter Five

SOLVING THE WILD HORSE PROBLEM

The BLM has set a goal of reducing the population of wild horses in the West to about 30,000 animals. In Nevada, the government is aiming for about 19,500 animals; in 1987, about 26,000 lived there. By mid 1988, over 100,000 wild horses and burros had been removed from the western states by the BLM. About 83,000 of these had been adopted through the Adopt-a-Horse program. Although the Wild Horse and Burro Act provided for destruction of unadopted animals, no healthy ones have been destroyed since 1982. Instead, as many as 10,000 are kept in holding pens, fed and cared for by the government. Because this costs about nine million dollars a year, the BLM would like to begin killing unadopted animals again. Congress, in 1987, forbade the BLM to use any government funds in 1988 to kill healthy wild horses.

HORSES VERSUS CATTLE

Several groups of citizens devoted to the well-being of wild horses oppose the BLM's plans. They are angry that the government gave in to the ranchers when it decided to reduce drastically the number of wild horses. They feel that the horses have just as much right to the land as the cattle because the land is public and belongs to everyone. Grazing their cattle there is a privilege of the ranchers, not a right. The wild horse protection groups want the ranchers to reduce the number of cattle they graze, too, if the number of horses is to be cut. Only if both introduced species are decreased will the land be able to recover from overgrazing, they say.

The horse protection groups also believe that the government is trying to reduce the number of wild horses too quickly. If the animals were gathered over a longer period of time, it would be easier to find adopters for them. The International Society for the Protection of Mustangs and Burros wants to see homes found for the horses the BLM is holding in pens before more horses are rounded up. With fewer horses available for adoption, the chances of adopting out those on hand would

Wild horses at Rock Springs, Wyoming.

be better. The BLM, however, doesn't always make the decisions. The courts have ordered the BLM to round up horses in some cases where the animals roam across private as well as public lands. This increases the number of wild horses being held, too.

Some groups, like the National Mustang Association, believe that there is room for more than 30,000 horses on the range. They would like to see more water sources developed and more effort spent on improving grazing so that fewer horses need to be captured.

THE ADOPT-A-HORSE PROGRAM

The Adopt-a-Horse program enables any adult who can properly care for a horse to take on a wild one for a $125 fee. The fee has remained the same for several years but could change, depending on the price of domesticated horses. If a mare has a foal at her side, both come together for the price of one. Prospective adopters must first fill out an application form, which allows them to adopt up to four horses. Then they go to a center, look over the animals, and choose what they want. There are permanent Adopt-a-Horse centers in the states with wild horses and also in Nebraska, Texas, Tennessee, and Pennsylvania. Temporary centers in other places also help make wild horses more widely available. Recently a new center was set up in Ohio.

For the first year, an adopted horse still belongs to the government. But after one year, if a veterinarian states that the horse has been well cared for, the adopter owns the horse and can keep it or sell it.

Pryor Mountain horses awaiting adoption.

Whoever adopts this mare will also get her foal.

Potential adopters look over the Pryor horses.

THE PROBLEM OF UNADOPTABLE HORSES

Unfortunately, it is almost impossible to find homes for some of the horses that are rounded up. Unlike the Pryor mustangs, many of the wild horses in other areas are not attractive, good-sized animals. Some have big heads and crooked legs and are not desirable as riding horses. In addition, horses that have been wild for many years, especially stallions, are often impossible to tame. An older stallion may never come to trust a human enough to let himself even be touched, much less ridden.

What can be done with these horses? Life in a pen, feeding on hay provided by people, hardly seems worthwhile for an animal used to freedom. Fortunately, some unadoptable horses now live in grassy pastures at a sanctuary in South Dakota established by the Institute of Range and the American Mustang. Eventually, this will be home for about 3,500 horses that otherwise would be doomed to life in confinement.

Unadoptable horses, such as older stallions, used to be adopted by ranchers with plenty of land. Before they

Stallions chosen for group adoption.

Roping a stallion.

were given to the ranchers, the stallions were gelded (their testicles were removed) so that they couldn't father foals in case they got loose among domesticated horses. They were given an obvious brand so that they could be easily identified. Then they were trucked to the ranch. After a year, when the rancher got free title to the horses, he could sell them at auction. Some horse protection groups got upset about these group adoptions. They knew that many of the horses, after their year of freedom roaming the ranch pastures, ended up being bought by dog-food factories or sent to other countries for human food. In April of 1988, such group adoptions were suspended by the BLM.

Another way to make the horses more desirable for adoption is to start the taming process before adopting them out. If the animal is already accustomed to being handled by people, it is more likely to develop into a useful riding horse. In Colorado, inmates at the state penitentiary in Canon City help tame wild horses. For about thirty days, the inmates work with each horse, teaching it to accept a halter and to trust people. The horses from Canon City usually find homes quickly. Because of the success in Colorado, California, New Mexico, and Wyoming have begun similar programs.

All captured wild horses receive a special brand on the neck that identifies them as adopted wild horses. The horses in a group adoption also get a more visible brand on the rump.

Ready to head for a new home.

CONTROLLING POPULATION GROWTH

Even after the BLM reduces the number of wild horses, the populations will need to be controlled in some way. In each area with wild horses, roundups will have to take place every three to five years to keep the numbers down if something else is not done.

One way to keep the population down is to prevent the animals from multiplying so quickly. Scientists are studying birth control methods for horses. One technique would involve injecting a hormone into harem stallions. The hormone reduces the sperm produced by the stallion so that he fathers many fewer foals than normal. There are problems with this method, however. When a mare does not get pregnant, she becomes ready to mate again. Another stallion, perhaps a less desirable one, could breed with her then.

Other scientists are testing a different, more promising method to lower the birth rate. They are capturing mares and inserting hormone capsules under their skin. The hormones act like birth control pills, preventing the mares from getting pregnant. If this method turns out to be practical and effective, it may help keep wild horse populations from growing so fast in the future.

A wild stallion.

A frightened wild horse may try to jump even a very high fence.

Chapter Six

TAMING THE WILD

Capturing and taming a wild horse has always had romantic appeal for Americans. Cowboys did it until the law protecting wild horses was passed in 1971, and many popular stories for children are based on this idea. To tame a wild horse and gain its trust seems to be the ultimate challenge for many horse lovers.

BECOMING TAME

Taming a wild horse is not an easy job. Wild horses are afraid of people, so the first step is to earn the animal's trust. Because they can jump high and will try to escape if frightened, the adopted horse should be placed in a sturdy pen with at least six-foot walls and no sharp edges. The horse needs peace and quiet, with no barking dogs or other disturbances to frighten it. It needs fresh water and fresh hay each day. If the same person always feeds the horse, it will come to trust that person bit by bit. It takes time for the horse to get used to its new owner and to learn that no harm will come to it.

Usually, weeks pass before a wild horse will allow a person to touch it. But once that trust has been established, the horse is on its way to becoming a member of the family. From then on, it can be carefully trained like a domestic horse, with patience and gentleness.

Several organizations offer help to people who adopt wild horses. The American Mustang and Burro Association gives advice on caring for adopted horses and burros. The North American Mustang Association and Registry brings owners and their adopted horses together for competition and fellowship.

THE SPANISH MUSTANG

While many different kinds of horses have gone free and produced today's wild horse, the very first were the Spanish mustangs. Their blood still flows in the veins of some wild horses. The romance of the mustang has led people to try to find horses that retain this old heritage. In 1920, Robert Brislawn and his brother Ferdinand began hunting for true mustangs among America's wild

Top: *This wild horse was adopted and successfully tamed by its new owner.* Bottom: *This wild-born foal, treated with gentle kindness, has now come to trust humans.*

A Spanish mustang.

horses. They found a few such horses among wild bands in several states and in herds on some Indian reservations. The Brislawns bred these animals carefully for years, doing autopsies after the horses died to make sure that the animals had the short backbone of a true mustang. In 1957, the Spanish Mustang Registry was established to help preserve this unique and special horse. The registry makes sure that only horses with the correct breeding are called Spanish mustangs by keeping records of the parentage of registered mustangs. The Southwest Spanish Mustang Association sponsors trail rides that show off the great endurance of these tough little horses.

The Spanish mustang is a hardy horse that is easy to care for. Its ancestors had to be strong, healthy, and intelligent to survive in the wild, and the tame Spanish mustang of today retains these traits.

THE TOUGH SURVIVORS

The Spanish mustang is just one example of the kind of horse that can be discovered among the wild horses of America. All these animals must be tough to survive the rigors of the wild. In parts of Nevada where wild horses roam, summer temperatures climb to over one hundred degrees, while in the winter the thermometer drops as low as forty degrees below zero. Water is scarce, and grass sparse. To survive in such a climate, horses must be very hardy and strong. Their toughness recalls the determination and courage of the human pioneers who bravely faced the challenges of the new land. By surviving the worst nature has to offer and thriving in freedom, wild horses remind us of the history and heritage of our country.

Wild Horse Organizations

The following organizations work for the protection of wild horses. They also have newsletters that keep members aware of recent news concerning wild horses. Some also are involved with other activities, as noted below:

American Horse Protection Association
1902-B T Street, N.W., Washington, DC 20009

American Mustang and Burro Association, Inc.
P.O. Box 216, Liberty Hill, TX 78642

> Helps the BLM with adoptions; has a wild horse and burro museum and library; is establishing sanctuaries for unadoptable animals. Sponsors activities such as trail rides and meetings for wild horse adopters.

International Society for the Protection
of Mustangs and Burros
11790 Deodar Way, Reno, NV 89506

> Sponsors a foster home care program for the place-
> ment and care of unadoptable wild horses and
> burros.

National Mustang Association, Inc.
1st and Main Street, Newcastle, UT 84756

> Helps the BLM with projects, such as developing
> water sources, which help wild horses; is setting up
> a sanctuary for unadoptable horses.

Institute of Range and the American Mustang
P.O. Box 932, Hot Springs, SD 57747

> Operates a sanctuary for unadoptable horses that is
> open to the public.

National Organization for Wild American Horses
P.O. Box 1719, Bailey, CO 80421

The following organizations are involved in registering
various types of horses derived from the American wild
horse:

American Indian Horse Registry
Rt. 3, Box 64, Lockhart, TX 78644

American Mustang Association
P.O. Box 338, Yucaipa, CA 92399

North American Mustang Association and Registry
8351 San Cristobal, Dallas, TX 75281

Southwest Spanish Mustang Association
P.O. Box 148, Finley, OK 74543

Spanish Mustang Registry, Inc.
8328 Stevenson Ave., Sacramento, CA 95828

Spanish-Barb Breeders Association
Box 485, 2888 Bluff St., Boulder, CO 80302

For information about adopting wild horses, contact:

Adopt-a-Horse,
Bureau of Land Management (130)
Room 5600
18th & C Streets, N.W., Washington, DC 20240

Index

Page numbers in *italics* refer to illustrations.

ABOUT THE AUTHOR

Dorothy Hinshaw Patent was born in Minnesota and grew up in Marin County, California. She received a Ph.D. in zoology from the University of California at Berkeley. She and her author/husband, Gregory, now live in Missoula, Montana. They have two grown sons. Dr. Patent has written more than forty-five books for children and young adults, most of which have been selected as Outstanding Science Trade Books for Children. Two of her books received awards from the Society of Children's Book Writers, and one, *Spider Magic,* was an American Library Association Notable Book for 1982. Most recently, Dr. Patent received the 1987 Eva L. Gordon Award for Children's Science Literature given by the American Nature Study Society in recognition of her many outstanding books for young readers.

ABOUT THE PHOTOGRAPHER

William Muñoz, a freelance photographer, has collaborated with Dr. Patent on many of her books. He received a B.A. in history from the University of Montana. He, his wife, Sandy, and their young son, Sean, live on a farm near St. Ignatius, Montana. Mr. Muñoz thoroughly enjoyed taking the photos for this book. "It took some time before the wild horses would tolerate my presence. But persistence paid off, and finally, one day, they didn't run at the sight of me with my camera. Eventually, I even got within fifteen feet of the animals!" Mr. Muñoz began photographing the wild horses at the Pryor Mountain range in 1982 and completed his work in 1987.